Essential Life Science

INHERITANCE AND REPRODUCTION

Jen Green

Raintree

Raintree is an imprint of Capstone Global Library Limited, a company incorporated in England and Wales having its registered office at 7 Pilgrim Street, London, EC4V 6LB – Registered company number: 6695582

www.raintreepublishers.co.uk
myorders@raintreepublishers.co.uk

Edited by Nancy Dickmann and Abby Colich
Designed by Rich Parker
Original illustrations © Capstone Global Library Ltd 2014
Illustrated by HL Studios
Picture research by Tracy Cummins
Originated by Capstone Global Library Ltd
Printed in China by China Translation and Printing Services

ISBN 978-1-4062-6227-8 (hardback)
17 16 15 14 13
10 9 8 7 6 5 4 3 2 1

ISBN 978-1-4062-6237-7 (paperback)
18 17 16 15 14
10 9 8 7 6 5 4 3 2 1

British Library Cataloguing in Publication Data
Green, Jen.
  Inheritance and reproduction. -- (Essential life science)
  1. Reproduction--Juvenile literature. 2. Inheritance of acquired characters--Juvenile literature.
  I. Title II. Series
  571.8-dc23

Acknowledgements
We would like to thank the following for permission to reproduce photographs: Capstone Library: pp. 14 (Karon Dubke), 15 (Karon Dubke), 40 (Karon Dubke); Getty Images: pp. 23 (Steve Allen), 26 bottom (Ed Reschke), 42 (Adam Gault), 43 (Chung Sung-Jun/Staff); istockphoto: p. 36 (© Nina Shannon); Photo Researchers, Inc.: pp. 6 (CNRI / Science Source), 7 (Science Source), 9 (Nigel Cattlin), 10 (Nigel Cattlin / Science Source), 12 (William Harlo), 13 (Nigel Cattlin), 18 (Perennou Nuridsany), 20 (Clem Haagner), 25 (Cosmos Blank); Shutterstock: pp. 4 (© worldswildlifewonders), 8 (© Sebastian Kaulitzki), 11 (© Daniel Prudek), 17 (© AndreAnita), 26 top (© NEIL ROY JOHNSON), 27 top (© Eric Isselée), 28 (© John L. Absher), 30 (© Marlon Lopez), 32 (© Bryan Busovicki), 34 (© Andresr), 35 (© AISPIX by Image Source), 38 (© Pete Saloutos), 39 (© wavebreakmedia), 41 bottom (© Yuri Arcurs), 41 top left (© Piotr Marcinski), 41 top right (© Tatjana Romanova); Superstock: pp. 5 (© age fotostock), 16 (© NHPA), 19 (© NaturePL), 21 (© age fotostock), 27 bottom (© Minden Pictures), 29 (© NHPA), 31 (© age fotostock).

Cover photograph of a ring tailed lemur reproduced with permission from Superstock (© J & C Sohns / Tier und Naturfotografie).

Every effort has been made to contact copyright holders of material reproduced in this book. Any omissions will be rectified in subsequent printings if notice is given to the publisher.

Disclaimer
All the internet addresses (URLs) given in this book were valid at the time of going to press. However, due to the dynamic nature of the internet, some addresses may have changed, or sites may have changed or ceased to exist since publication. While the author and publisher regret any inconvenience this may cause readers, no responsibility for any such changes can be accepted by either the author or the publisher.

Contents

Eureka moment!

Learn about important discoveries that have brought about further knowledge and understanding.

DID YOU KNOW?

Discover fascinating facts about inheritance and reproduction.

WHAT'S NEXT?

Read about the latest research and advances in essential life science.

Some words are shown in bold, **like this**. You can find out what they mean by looking in the glossary.

What are inheritance and reproduction?

What do a mouse and a mighty oak tree have in common? They are both living things, that are born, grow, and later die. While they are **mature** or grown-up, they produce young, so that when they die, their **species** continues. **Reproduction** is the amazing process by which living things produce young. It happens in many different ways. Without reproduction there would be no life on Earth!

New life is starting all the time. As you read this, baby birds are hatching from eggs. Human babies are being born. Young plants are sprouting from seeds.

Young animals look like their parents because of genes. That's why this young koala has a black nose and round ears, like its mother.

Cells, genes, and inheritance

All living things are made of tiny units called **cells**. Some very simple living things are made of just one cell. Your body has many billions of cells. Inside every cell are sets of instructions called **genes**. These work like plans, providing the information that tells living thing how to grow and develop. Genes are vital to **inheritance**, which is the process through which living things pass on features such as hair and skin colour to their young.

DID YOU KNOW?

A plant or animal's **life cycle** is all the stages it passes through as it grows, produces young, and dies. Some species complete their life cycle in just a few weeks. Others take years or even centuries. House flies live for just 15 to 25 days. Mice live about eighteen months. Pet cats can live for about 20 years. Humans live for 70-90 years. A yew tree lives for thousands of years.

Beech trees develop from seeds. The seed contains instructions that tell the plant to grow into a beech tree, not another type of tree.

How do living things reproduce?

There are two main types of reproduction, **sexual** and **asexual reproduction**. Most plants and animals reproduce sexually. A male and female pair up to have young. Some living things reproduce asexually, without a mate. Very simple life forms such as **bacteria** are made of a single cell. They reproduce by dividing. The cell splits to form two cells, which then grow and divide again.

This bacterium is reproducing by dividing in two. Each new bacterium is an exact copy of the original.

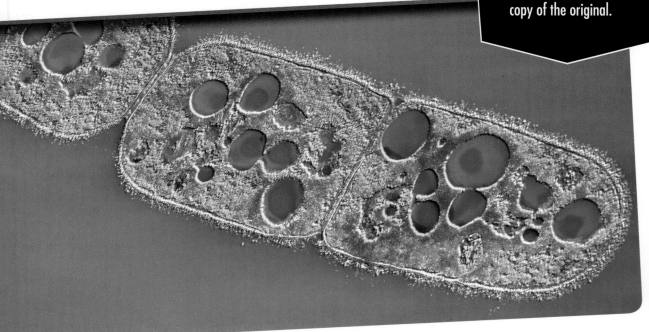

Buds and runners

Some living things that have many cells also reproduce asexually. A hydra is a tiny pond animal. A growth called a bud appears on the hydra's body. It grows and splits off to become a young hydra. The baby is an exact copy of its parent, called a **clone**.

Like most plants, strawberry plants reproduce sexually by making seeds. But they can also reproduce asexually by developing stems called runners. The runners grow away from the parent and eventually put down roots to become new plants.

▷
DID YOU KNOW?

Starfish have five arms. If one arm breaks off, a starfish can grow a new one. In some species, a broken-off arm can grow a whole body to become a new starfish. But they usually reproduce sexually.

A hydra reproduces by growing a small copy of itself, which then splits off.

Eureka moment!

For a long time, no one knew about genes or understood inheritance. The first step was the discovery of cells. In around 1600, scientists made the first microscopes. This allowed them to see small creatures such as fleas larger than lifesize. Later more powerful microscopes were made. These allowed scientists to look inside cells.

Sexual reproduction

Most plants and animals reproduce sexually. Males produce male sex cells called **sperm**. Females produce female sex cells called **ova**, or **eggs**. New life begins when a sperm joins with an ovum (egg) to fertilize it. Both cells carry genes, so the young inherit features from both parents. The fertilized egg then grows and develops into a baby animal or plant.

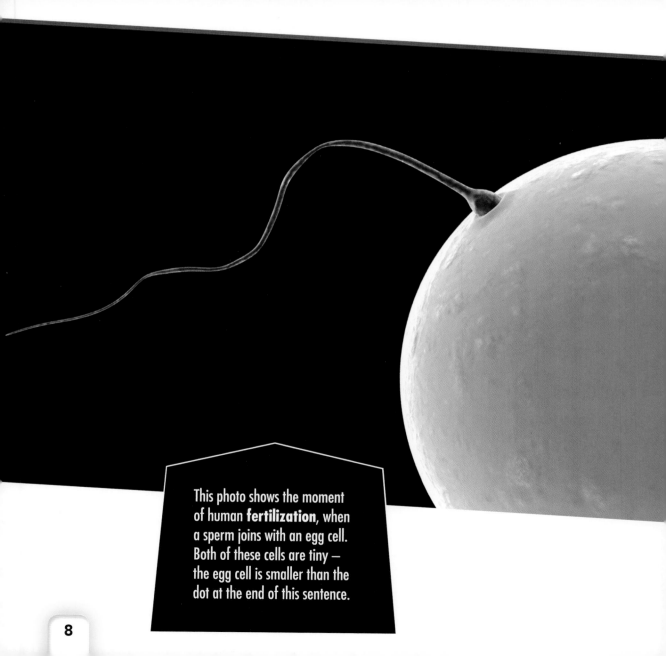

This photo shows the moment of human **fertilization**, when a sperm joins with an egg cell. Both of these cells are tiny — the egg cell is smaller than the dot at the end of this sentence.

Both sexes in one

Most animals are either male or female, but earthworms are both! Each worm can make both sperm and eggs. However, earthworms still need to **mate** to produce young. As they mate, they swap male cells, which fertilize each other's eggs. Animals that are both male and female are called **hermaphrodites**. Being both sexes makes it easier to find a partner. This increases the chance of having young.

DID YOU KNOW?

Most animals reproduce either sexually or asexually. But insects called aphids have a life cycle that involves both kinds of reproduction. In spring, females hatch from eggs. They grow up very quickly and can reproduce without mating, producing many generations. Almost all of the young are female, but males are also born in late summer. The males and females mate. The females lay fertilized eggs, which will hatch out the following spring.

Young aphids are clones — exact copies of the mother. Asexual reproduction allows aphids to reproduce very quickly in summer.

How do plants make seeds?

Flowering plants reproduce by making seeds. But before they can do so, their flowers must be fertilized by **pollen** from another flower of the same kind. Male sex cells in the pollen fertilize the female sex cells, called **ova**. This process is called **pollination**.

Most flowers contain both male and female parts. The male part, the **stamens**, make pollen. The female part, called the **carpel**, contains the ova.

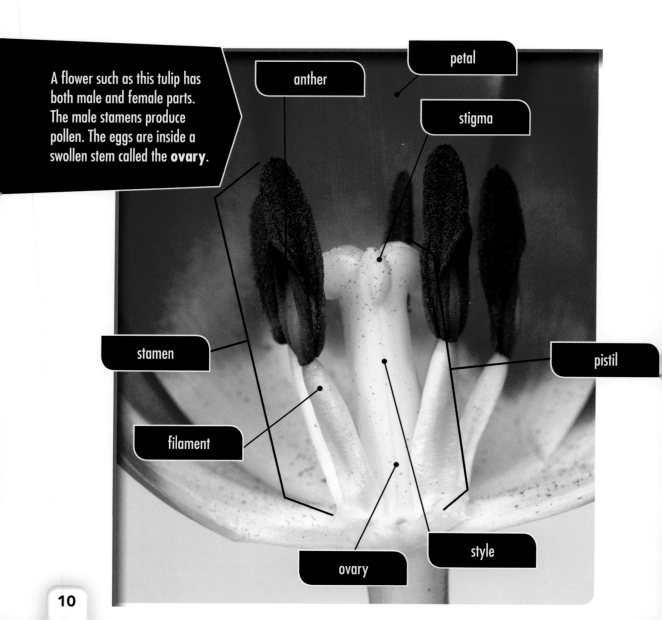

A flower such as this tulip has both male and female parts. The male stamens produce pollen. The eggs are inside a swollen stem called the **ovary**.

petal

anther

stigma

stamen

pistil

filament

style

ovary

Spreading pollen

Some plants produce very light pollen, which drifts on the wind to other flowers. Other plants rely on insects, birds, or bats to spread their pollen. Their flowers are brightly coloured and hold a sweet drink called nectar. The colours and scents attract insects such as bees.

Honeybees visit flowers to gather pollen and nectar for food. As the bee reaches into the flower, dusty pollen grains stick to its hairy body. The grains rub off onto the next plant the bee visits, to pollinate the flowers. Male sex cells from the pollen unite with the egg cells, to fertilize the plant.

WHAT'S NEXT?

Honeybees help farmers and gardeners by pollinating crops and fruit trees. But lately bees have not been doing well, and many bee colonies have died. Scientists are trying to work out what is wrong, so we can put it right. Without bees, crops such as apples, almonds, and pumpkins could fail.

Bees transfer pollen as they fly from flower to flower.

Fruit protection

Flowering plants develop seeds once they have been fertilized. The seeds develop inside the ovary at the base of the flower, which swells to form a fruit. The fruit protects the growing seeds. Fruits can be either juicy berries or a dry nut, bean, or pod.

Witch hazel capsules burst open to scatter their seeds.

Spreading seeds

Ripe seeds need light and moisture to sprout, or **germinate**. So they need to get away from the parent plant that would shade them and take their moisture. Some seeds blow away on the wind, others are carried by water.

Many plants rely on animals to spread their seeds. Animals eat the fruit containing the seeds. The seeds pass unharmed through the animal's body, and are left in another place in its droppings. If a seed falls in a moist, sunny position in fertile soil, it will germinate. The seed case splits open. A little root grows down to absorb water. A green shoot grows upwards and spreads its leaves. The young plant begins to make its own food using sunlight energy. Eventually when it is well grown, it will produce its own seeds. This completes the plant's life cycle.

A germinating maize seedling develops a root and a green shoot.

Eureka moment!

Modern crops such as wheat have been developed from wild plants, which originally produced small seeds. In prehistoric times, people discovered that the seeds, or grains, could be used to make flour and bread. Each year, farmers saved the biggest seeds to sow next year. Over time, the wild plants developed into modern crops, which produce large grains, for bumper harvests.

Try this!

Investigate the life cycle of flowering plants by growing your own sunflowers in spring. These plants grow well in a flowerbed or in a large pot or window box. Sunflowers grow really fast and can tower over 3 metres (10 feet) tall!

What you need
- packet of sunflower seeds
- trowel
- large pot
- potting compost
- canes
- string

What you do:

1 Fill a pot with potting compost to within 2.5 cm (1 in) of the top. Water the soil. Push the seeds into the soil to a depth of 5 cm (2 in). Plant seeds at least 10 cm (4 in) apart. Put the pot in a sunny position on a windowsill.

2 After one or two weeks, the seeds will germinate to produce seedlings. Remove weak seedlings to allow the others space to grow. Water the plants regularly. Move the pot outside as the plants grow bigger.

3 When the plants are about 30 cm (1 ft) tall, push a cane into the soil by each plant. Tie the stem to the cane with string. As the plants grow taller, tie them higher up. Continue to water regularly.

Seeds grow in the centre of the large flower head.

4 After about two months the flowers develop and open. Watch how the flower heads turn to face the sun, which helps the seeds to ripen. Save some seeds to grow next year.

5 Make a chart to record plant growth and stages in the plant's life cycle. Measure the plant's height each week and record any changes you see. Draw pictures or take photographs. Measure the flower heads. You could hold a competition with your friends to see who can grow the tallest sunflower.

How do animals have young?

Animals that reproduce sexually must first find a partner. They use different signals to attract a mate. Animals such as frogs and deer use sounds, such as croaks or roaring noises. Other creatures use scent. Female moths give off a very powerful smell that male moths can pick up from 1.6 km (one mile) away.

A stag (male deer) roars to announce he is ready to mate. His roaring warns off other males and attracts females.

Some animals put on displays to attract a partner. A male peacock spreads his beautiful tail to attract the female. All of these signals are a way of telling other members of the species that the animal is ready to mate.

DID YOU KNOW?

Among animals that rely on sight to find a mate, it is usually the males that are bigger and more brightly coloured. This is because the females get the final say about who to mate with. They choose the biggest and strongest males as mates. Male animals such as stags and hippos fight for the chance to mate.

Fertilization

Life begins at the moment of fertilization, when the sperm unites with the egg cell. In many fish, frogs, and other water-dwelling animals, this happens in water. The female fish releases her eggs, then the male spreads his sperm over them. In mammals, birds, and other animals that live on land, fertilization happens inside the female's body.

The fertilized egg cell divides many times to form a ball of cells, which develops into an **embryo**. As the embryo develops, genes in its cells provide instructions that are needed for special cells to develop. These then form body parts such as legs, wings, and tail.

Cranes dance to get to know one another before mating.

Laying eggs

Most animals including fish, reptiles, birds, and insects reproduce by laying eggs. There are two types of eggs. Fish, frogs, and other water animals produce soft, tiny eggs called **spawn**. They lay hundreds or even thousands of eggs at one time. Almost all will be eaten by other animals, but a few survive to grow, develop, become adult, and reproduce.

A male toad wraps eggs around its legs to protect them until they hatch into tadpoles.

The eggs that birds and reptiles lay are much larger and more developed. They are made of many cells and have a hard or tough, leathery shell to protect the baby developing inside. They also contain a **yolk**, which provides food for the baby.

Caring for eggs

As a general rule, birds and reptiles produce far fewer eggs than fish or frogs, and take good care of them. Reptiles protect their eggs by burying them in sand or vegetation. Birds build nests to protect their eggs. They sit on the eggs to keep them warm while they develop. When the baby is fully formed it hatches, or breaks out of its shell.

A baby tortoise breaks out of its shell using a hard tip on its nose.

WHAT'S NEXT?

Sea turtles swim to quiet beaches to **breed**. After mating, the female comes ashore. She digs a hole in the sand and lays her eggs there, covering them with sand. When the babies hatch, they dig themselves out and head down to the water. However, these quiet beaches are being taken over by holiday-makers. The noise disturbs the turtles. In future if there are no quiet beaches, turtles will have nowhere to lay eggs.

Mammal reproduction

Most mammals reproduce in a way that is different to other animals. Instead of laying eggs, the young of most mammals develop in a part of the body called the **womb** inside the mother. The baby gets food and oxygen from its mother through an **organ** called the **placenta**. When it is developed enough to survive outside the womb, it is born.

Most baby mammals are born well developed. This baby zebra can stand just a few minutes after birth.

Marsupials

Kangaroos and opossums are **marsupials**. Instead of being born well developed, these babies are born when they are still very tiny. The helpless baby crawls up its mother's fur into a pouch on her belly. There it sucks its mother's milk. It stays in the pouch for months, until it is big and strong.

Baby kangaroos stay in the pouch until they are six months old.

Egg-laying mammals

A very few mammals reproduce by laying eggs, that look like reptile eggs. The duck-billed platypus lays her eggs in a burrow. The echidna carries her egg or eggs in a pouch. Both of these animals live in Australia.

DID YOU KNOW?

The time between fertilisation and birth is called **gestation**. Gestation times vary among mammals. Baby mice are born after 20 days, baby cats and dogs after nine weeks. Baby kangaroos are born after just five weeks, human babies after nine months. Baby whales spend a year in the womb. Baby elephants spend 22 months – the longest time of all.

Human reproduction

Humans develop in a similar way to most other mammals. Like all mammals you began life as a fertilized egg cell inside your mother. As the ball of cells divided, cells of different types developed. These grouped together to make body parts such as heart, brain, and lungs.

You grew in your mother's womb, where the placenta provided food and oxygen. This nourishment passed into your body through a tube, which ended at your belly button. When you were born this cord was cut.

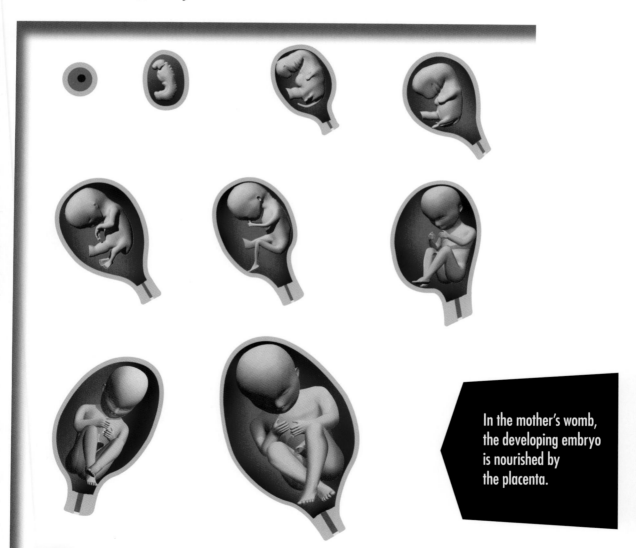

In the mother's womb, the developing embryo is nourished by the placenta.

Growing and developing

After one month in the womb, an embryo is only the size of a baked bean. Its heart starts beating. After two months, it starts to look more human, with arms and legs complete with fingers and toes. After four months, features such as eyes, nose, mouth, hair, and nails have formed.

Five months after fertilization, most mothers can feel their unborn baby kicking. After eight months, the **foetus's** lungs are developed, ready to start breathing. Most babies are born after nine months. Normally, muscles in the womb tighten to push the baby out.

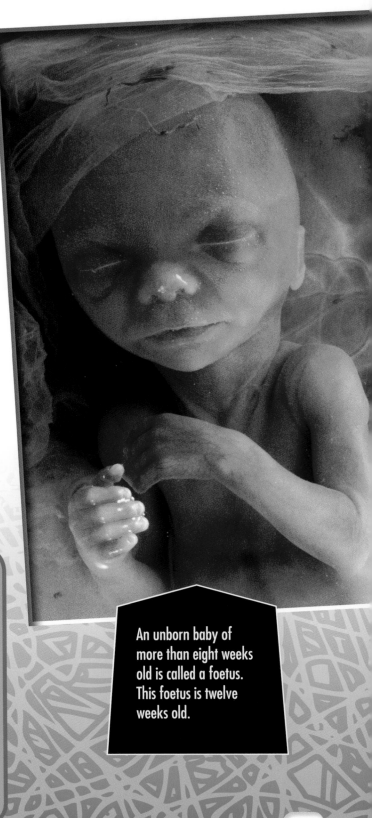

An unborn baby of more than eight weeks old is called a foetus. This foetus is twelve weeks old.

WHAT'S NEXT?

A special test called an **ultrasound scan** allows doctors and parents to see the unborn baby in the womb. Doctors use ultrasound to check the baby's health and development. In future, ultrasound will allow doctors to carry out surgery on unborn babies if needed.

How do young animals grow?

Animals travel through their life cycle as they grow into adults and have young of their own. All animals change shape as they grow up, but some change a lot more than others.

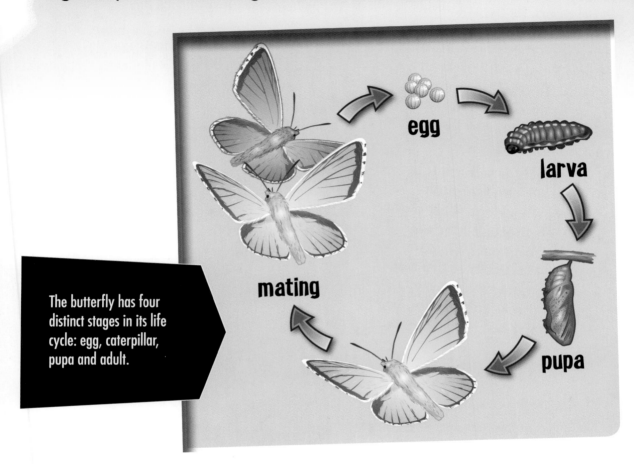

egg

larva

pupa

mating

The butterfly has four distinct stages in its life cycle: egg, caterpillar, pupa and adult.

Dramatic change

Animals such as butterflies pass through very dramatic changes as they grow. Butterflies lay their eggs after mating. After a week, the eggs hatch into caterpillars, which look nothing like the adults. The caterpillar feeds and grows very quickly. When fully grown, it makes a silk case for itself and becomes a **pupa**. Inside the hard case, its body breaks down and is rebuilt. Eventually the winged butterfly comes out and flies off to find a mate.

Small changes

Other young animals grow up much more gradually. A newly-hatched baby snake looks a lot like its mother, only smaller. It feeds and grows. Whenever its skin gets too tight, it wriggles out of it. This is called **moulting**. When fully grown it looks for a mate.

A young snake moults its skin. The new skin underneath is stretchy, with room to grow.

▷ DID YOU KNOW?

Insects spend different amounts of time at various stages in their life cycle. A red admiral butterfly spends a week as an egg, five weeks as a caterpillar, two weeks as a pupa and nine months as an adult. A periodical cicada spends 17 years growing up underground, and less than a month as an adult. A mayfly spends two years growing up in the pond, and just 12 hours as an adult.

Try this!

A frog has several stages in its life cycle. It hatches from an egg into a water-dwelling tadpole, which slowly turns into an adult frog, that lives on land. These amazing changes take place over about three months in spring.

What you need

- glass jar
- magnifying glass
- rubber boots (wellingtons)

Warning: Always take great care near water. Take a trusted adult to keep you safe.

Visit your local pond each week to observe the frog's life cycle. Use a glass jar to scoop water containing tadpoles out of the pond. Study the tadpoles with a magnifying glass, keeping the jar out of the sun. Then put them back gently. Don't keep them out of the pond for long.

What you'll see

(1) In spring frogs visit ponds to breed. The females lay jelly-coated eggs, which are fertilized by the males. The black dot at the centre of each egg will develop into a tadpole. Notice how the eggs develop.

(2) After two to three weeks, tadpoles hatch from the eggs. They are legless with long tails. Notice how they swim. Tadpoles breathe using feathery **gills** on their heads. You can see these using a magnifying glass. What do tadpoles eat?

3 After about five weeks, tadpoles develop legs – the back legs first, then the front legs. The lungs are also developing. You may see tadpoles start to gulp air at the surface.

4 After 11 weeks, the tadpole's tail shrinks as it changes into a **froglet**. It is now breathing air and spending time out of the water. Don't pick up the froglets at this stage, but notice what they are eating. How do they catch their food?

Record each stage of the frog's life cycle in a notebook. Note the date of each visit. Notice and record the size at each stage. Notice how the animal moves, breathes, and feeds. Make drawings and label parts such as gills and legs.

Taking care of young

Most animals don't look after their young. Most fish, reptiles, and insects simply lay their eggs in a safe place where food is plentiful, and then move on. They lay a lot of eggs that mostly die, but a few survive to carry on the species. Birds and mammals are different. They have far fewer babies and take much more care of them. This gives the young a better chance of survival.

A thrush parent brings food for its hungry babies.

Caring parents

Birds are good parents. Baby birds born in a nest are called **nestlings**. At first they are quite helpless, being blind and without feathers. They rely on their parents to bring food. Soon their eyes open and their feathers grow. In a few weeks they are ready to leave the nest and take care of themselves.

Mammals take even more care of their young. Baby mammals such as foals are quickly on their feet, but most are helpless, like nestlings. The first food of all baby mammals is their mother's milk. As the baby grows, the mother teaches vital skills such as how to find food and avoid danger. Some young mammals grow up faster than others. Mice leave the nest after just three weeks. Young whales, elephants, and chimpanzees stay with their families for years, learning how to survive.

A young bonobo learns to use a stone as a hammer by copying an adult.

Eureka moment!

In 1960, a young scientist named Jane Goodall noticed African chimpanzees using tools. Before that, people thought that only humans were clever enough to use tools. Later she discovered that young chimps learn to use tools by watching and copying the adults.

From child to adult

Humans spend more time growing up than other animals. This may be because we have more to learn. Human babies are as helpless as newborn puppies and kittens. As a newborn baby, you couldn't stand or even hold your head up. But you knew to cry when you were cold or hungry.

Growing up

Learning comes slowly at first. At six months, most babies can sit up. By nine months, many babies learn to crawl. By the age of one or so, most children say their first words and take their first steps. Between one and ten years old, bodies change slowly but surely, as they get taller and legs and arms grow longer. Children learn hundreds of new skills, from reading and writing to using a computer.

Most children learn to walk around age one.

Becoming adult

Between the ages of ten and fourteen, human bodies change fast as they become adults. This time is called **puberty**. At ten or eleven, a girl's breasts develop, and she starts to have periods. Puberty happens a little later in boys. Between twelve and fourteen, a boy gets taller and more muscular. His voice gets deeper and hair grows on his body. After puberty you are able to have children of your own, but it's better to wait until you are older. Learning carries on right through life.

WHAT'S NEXT?

Humans live longer than most other mammals, thanks to modern medicine. A few centuries ago, most people did not live beyond 50. Now it's not unusual to live to 80 or even 90. The oldest human, Jeanne Calment, lived to the age of 122 years. In future, people might live even longer.

Learning a complicated skill such as riding a bicycle takes a lot of practice.

How do genes work?

Have you ever been told you look like your mum or dad? You look like your parents because features such as eye colour pass from parents to their children. This is called inheritance, and it happens through genes.

What are genes?

Genes are found inside cells. They are located in the cell **nucleus** – the tiny dot near the centre of each cell that controls how it works. Genes are like little bits of code. Each gene carries instructions for a particular feature, such as whether your hair is straight or curly. A full set of genes provides the instructions needed for building a unique living thing, such as you.

This cheetah looks like its parents because of genes.

Chromosomes and DNA

Inside the nucleus of each cell, genes are found inside long strings called **chromosomes**. These strings often coil up to make tiny X-shapes. You have 46 chromosomes in each cell, and each contains thousands of genes.

Genes are made of chemicals called **DNA**. DNA has an amazing shape, like a twisted ladder. The ladder's rungs are made up of four chemicals, which pair up in different ways. The arrangement forms a code that tells cells how to develop.

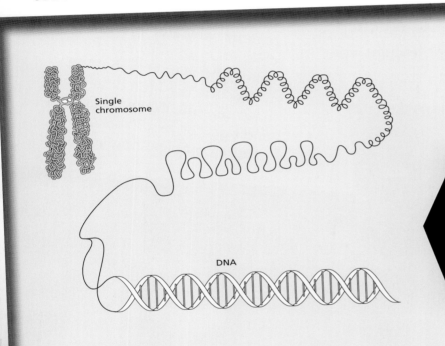

Single chromosome

DNA

Chromosomes are found inside cells. Genes are parts of chromosomes. They are made of DNA, which is shaped like a twisted ladder.

Eureka moment!

DNA was discovered in the 1940s, but no one knew what it looked like. Then in 1952, British scientist Rosalind Franklin managed to take photos of DNA. Two other scientists, Francis Crick and James Watson, used Franklin's photos to work out that DNA is shaped like a twisted ladder.

How does inheritance work?

So exactly how do genes pass on features from parents to their children? Well, remember that humans have 46 chromosomes. Nearly all the cells in your body have a full set of 46 chromosomes, but sperm and egg cells are different. They only have half the normal number: 23 chromosomes. When the sperm and egg cell join, each adds 23 chromosomes to make a full set of 46 in the fertilized egg. That's how you inherit features from both your mum and dad.

You inherit half your chromosomes from each parent. The exact combination is different every time.

Brothers and sisters

If children inherit 23 chromosomes from both their parents, why aren't all the children in a family exactly alike? The answer is that the DNA code is a little different in each sex cell. When the sperm and egg cell join it makes a unique combination each time.

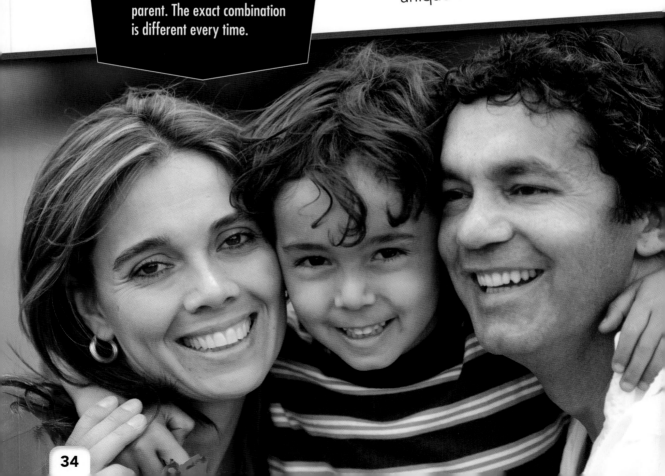

Boy or girl?

Whether you are a boy or girl is decided by a pair of chromosomes called sex chromosomes. The mother always adds an X chromosome, half the code for a girl. The father's chromosome may be another X, or a Y chromosome, the code for a boy. If he adds an X the baby will be a girl. If he adds a Y the child will be a boy.

This girl developed from a fertilized cell containing two X chromosomes. Her brother developed from a cell with one X and Y chromosome.

Strong and weak genes

Genes come in pairs, one from each parent. The two genes in a pair control the same feature, such as the colour of your hair. But because one gene comes from the mother and one from the father, the two may contain different information. For example, one may contain the code for dark hair, the other the code for fair hair. If you inherit the dark-hair gene from one parent and the fair-hair gene from the other, you will have dark hair. This is because the dark-hair gene is stronger than the fair-hair one. The stronger gene "wins". Strong genes are called **dominant genes**. Weak genes are called **recessive**.

The gene for dimples is stronger than the one for no-dimples. So if you inherit one of each gene from your parents, you will have dimples.

The fair-hair gene doesn't disappear altogether. It's still there but as it's weak, it doesn't make the hair its colour. However, if you grow up and marry a dark-haired partner who also has the fair-hair gene, one of your children could be fair, even though you both have dark hair. Both of you must pass on the fair hair gene for this to happen.

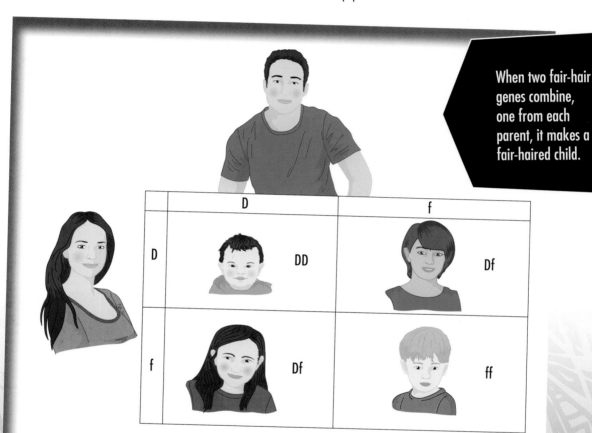

When two fair-hair genes combine, one from each parent, it makes a fair-haired child.

	D	f
D	DD	Df
f	Df	ff

Eureka moment!

The idea of strong and weak genes was discovered by an Austrian monk called Gregor Mendel in the 1860s. Mendel discovered how inheritance works by breeding pea plants in his monastery garden. He crossed plants that produced purple and white flowers and worked out that the purple-flower gene was stronger than the white one.

Do genes alone control how we develop?

Differences in our genes make each one of us unique. However genes don't have the whole say in what we look like and how we develop. Our surroundings and experiences also play a part. For example, you may inherit the gene for tallness from your parents, but you still need to eat a healthy diet to reach your full height.

Your body shape is affected by your genes, but also by what you eat and how active you are. Exercise and eating the right foods can help your muscles to develop. For example, a cyclist develops strong leg muscles through regular training. Dancers keep slim and fit by practising every day. On the other hand, eating too much sugary and fatty foods and not taking enough exercise can make you overweight.

Whatever your genes, you need to eat a balanced diet and exercise regularly to keep in shape.

Genes can give you musical ability. But you still need to practise to play well.

Ability and practice

Your genes may give you certain in-built talents, but you still need to develop them through practice. For example, you may inherit a gene that makes you musical, but you will still need a lot of practice to play well.

Eureka moment!

In the 1970s scientists learned how to alter the genes of living things. This is called **genetic modification** or **GM** for short. Modification means change. It is done by taking DNA from one living thing and putting it into another. In some countries, GM is used to produce crops with a special feature, for example strawberries that taste sweeter and melons that stay fresh for longer. However some people do not think this is a good idea.

Try this!

Do a survey to find out how features such as hair and eye colour are passed down in your family. Features such as freckles, dimples, straight or curly hair, and the shape of earlobes can be traced quite easily. Choose just two or three features. Make a chart to record the results.

What you need
- large sheet of paper
- photos of family members

What you do

1 Choose a feature such as eye colour. What colour are your eyes? What colour are the eyes of your mum and dad, brothers and sisters? What about your grandparents? You may need to ask your parents or look at photos to find out.

2 Make a family tree like the one shown here with your grandparents at the top, your parents in the middle and you, your brothers and sisters at the bottom. Add photos or drawings. Record details such as eye colour beside each family member.

3 Do the same again with another feature, such as the shape of your earlobes. Some people have small earlobes, that are attached to the sides of the head. Others have long, dangly earlobes.

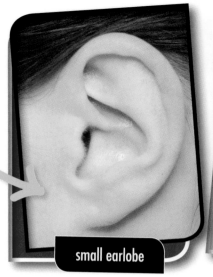

small earlobe

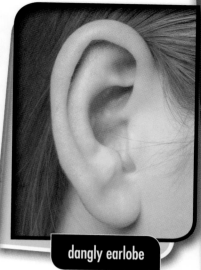

dangly earlobe

4 The table of strong and weak genes will help you to understand how features have passed down in your family. Can you draw any more conclusions about strong and weak genes by looking at the chart?

Feature	Strong	Weak
Eye colour	Brown eyes	Blue, green, or hazel eyes
Hair colour	Dark hair	Fair or red hair
Hair type	Straight	Curly
Earlobes	Dangly	Small, attached
Dimples	Dimples	No dimples
Freckles	Freckles	No freckles

This photograph of children, parents, and grandparents shows a strong family resemblance.

What next for inheritance and reproduction?

A few centuries ago many people were interested in reproduction, but no one understood inheritance. Farmers had developed new varieties of crops and animals by breeding from their best stock. This worked, but no one understood how features were passed on.

Genes and DNA

In the late 1800s, scientists began to understand how features such as height and colour were inherited. In the 1900s, they realised that inheritance happens through genes – strings of chemicals found inside cells. Genes are part of X-shaped structures called chromosomes. In time, scientists realised that genes were made of DNA, which acts like a code.

Scientists have produced tomatoes that don't go mouldy, by altering their genes.

In the future

In the 1970s, scientists learned how to change the genes of living things. Gene science has now been used to produce new types of animals and plants, including crops. In future, it will be used to cure inherited diseases and make medicines. Advances in medicine have been used to help couples who find it hard to have children. Gene science and medicine are changing so quickly there will be many new discoveries in your lifetime.

Gene science can be controversial. Scientists have produced clones (exact copies) of animals such as cats, dogs, pigs, and sheep. In the future it could be used to save endangered species. Human clones may be possible, but many people think this is taking science a step too far.

Eureka moment!

Doctors can now fertilize a mother's egg cell outside her body. The fertilized egg is then put back into the womb. This can help some mothers to get pregnant. This technique was used for the first time in 1978. Many babies have now been born in this way.

These dogs are all clones of one another.

Glossary

asexual reproduction when living things reproduce without a mate

bacterium (plural: bacteria) tiny, single-celled living thing

breed to mate and have young

carpel female part of a flower

cell one of the tiny units of which living things are made

chromosome x-shaped structure found inside cells, which contains genes

clone living thing that is an exact copy of another

DNA strings of chemicals inside cells that make up genes, and form a code

dominant gene strong gene, which will overrule the weaker gene with which it is paired

egg see ovum

embryo unborn human baby that is less than eight weeks old

fertilization moment when the male sex cell joins with the female egg, to start a new life

foetus unborn human baby developing in the womb, which is more than eight weeks old

froglet young frog

gene section of DNA that carries an inherited feature, such as eye or hair colour

genetic modification (GM) process of changing the genes of living things, so that they develop differently

germinate when a seed sprouts and starts to grow

gestation time between fertilization and birth, when a mother is pregnant

gill feathery structure on a fish or tadpole which the animal uses to breathe

hermaphrodite living thing that is both male and female

inheritance process through which features are passed on from parents to children

life cycle all the stages a living thing passes through in its lifetime, as it is born, grows and develops, breeds, and eventually dies

marsupial mammal such as a kangaroo, whose young are born early and develop in the mother's pouch

mate come together to breed and create young

mature when living things are able to reproduce

moulting when an animal sheds its skin

nestling baby bird born in a nest

nucleus control centre of a cell

organ body part with a particular job to do

ovary organ that produces eggs in female plants and animals

ovum (plural: ova) female sex cell or egg

pollen tiny grains that contain the male sex cells of plants

placenta blood-rich organ that develops in the womb to nourish the unborn baby

pollination when pollen is transferred from the male part of a plant to the female part, so that fertilization can take place

puberty stage in a human life cycle when the reproductive organs start working

pupa stage in an insect's life cycle between a larva and an adult

recessive gene weaker gene, which is overruled by a strong or dominant gene

reproduction process through which living things have young

sexual reproduction when a male and female living thing produce young

spawn tiny eggs of fish, frogs, and other water creatures.

species particular type of plant, animal, or other living thing

sperm male sex cell

stamen male part of a flower that produces pollen

ultrasound scan special test that uses sound waves to produce a picture of an unborn baby in the womb

womb organ inside the mother in which the baby develops

yolk part of an egg that nourishes developing young such as birds

Find out more

Books

Cells and Reproduction, Jen Green (Franklin Watts, 2008)

Human Reproduction (Sci-Hi), Casey Rand (Raintree, 2009)

Plant Reproduction (The Life of Plants), Louise and Richard Spilsbury (Heinemann, 2009)

Reproduction and Genetics (The Human Machine), Richard Spilsbury (Heinemann, 2009)

The Reproductive System (Body Focus), Steve Parker (Heinemann, 2010)

Websites

http://www.amnh.org/explore/ology/genetics

The American Museum of Natural History explains genetics.

www.bbc.co.uk/bitesize/ks2/science/living_things/life_cycles/play/

Find out more about life cycles.

www.bbc.co.uk/schools/gcsebitesize/science/21c_pre_2011/genetics/

BBC Bitesize has facts about genes and inheritance.

www.nlm.nih.gov/medlineplus/ency/article/002398.htm

This site shows how a human baby develops in the womb.

Places to visit

The Science Museum, London, UK
Learn about all areas of science and technology.

The American Museum of Natural History, New York, USA
This museum houses more than 32 million specimens and artefacts.

Australian Museum; Sydney, Australia
The oldest museum in Australia, explore natural history and indigenous cultures.

Zoos are great places to find more about animals. Find out about the nearest zoo at your library or on the Internet.

Further research

If you enjoyed this book, you might like to find out more about one of these topics:

The life cycle of plants

The life cycle of animals

How human babies develop

Genes and DNA

Use these books and websites to do more research. Visit one of the museums mentioned or your local library to find out more.

Index

BRIGHT
IDEA
BOOKS

AMAZING
Mountains
AROUND
THE WORLD

by Pat Tanumihardja

raintree

Raintree is an imprint of Capstone Global Library Limited, a company incorporated in England and Wales having its registered office at 264 Banbury Road, Oxford, OX2 7DY – Registered company number: 6695582

www.raintree.co.uk
myorders@raintree.co.uk

Edited by Claire Vanden Branden
Designed by Becky Daum
Original illustrations © Capstone Global Library Limited 2020
Production by Dan Peluso
Originated by Capstone Global Library Ltd
Printed and bound in India

ISBN 978 1 4747 7465 9 (hardback)
ISBN 978 1 4747 8118 3 (paperback)

British Library Cataloguing in Publication Data
A full catalogue record for this book is available from the British Library.

Acknowledgements
We would like to thank the following for permission to reproduce photographs: Alamy: Lunar Imagens, 14–15; iStockphoto: Jef Folkerts, 5, 28, LeoPatrizi, 9, oversnap, 13, rcaucino, 6–7, Sidekick, 30–31, squashedbox, 21, Zzvet, cover; Science Source: Krafft, 23; Shutterstock Images: EastVillage Images, 24–25, Gary Saxe, 18–19, Mariusz S. Jurgielewicz, 17, Richard A McMillin, 27, Vixit, 10, 10–11.

Every effort has been made to contact copyright holders of material reproduced in this book. Any omissions will be rectified in subsequent printings if notice is given to the publisher.

CONTENTS

CHAPTER 1

AMAZING
Mountains

Mountains are made from rock. They take a very long time to form.

Earth is made up of layers. The surface layer of Earth is called the crust. It is broken into huge pieces called **plates**.

Plates are always slowly moving. Sometimes one plate pushes underneath another. This lifts one plate up to form a mountain **range**. Sometimes plates push into each other. This is another way that mountains are formed.

Mountains can take thousands of years to form.

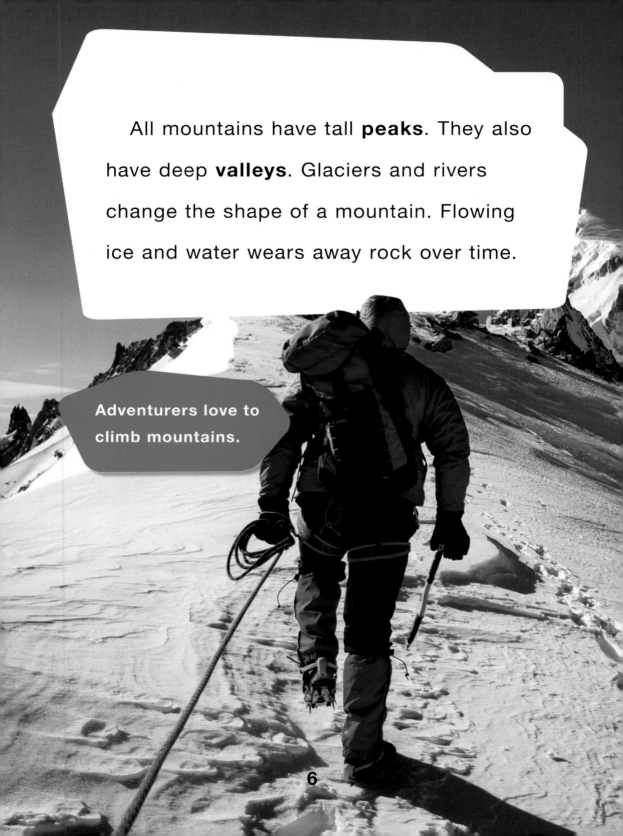

All mountains have tall **peaks**. They also have deep **valleys**. Glaciers and rivers change the shape of a mountain. Flowing ice and water wears away rock over time.

Adventurers love to climb mountains.

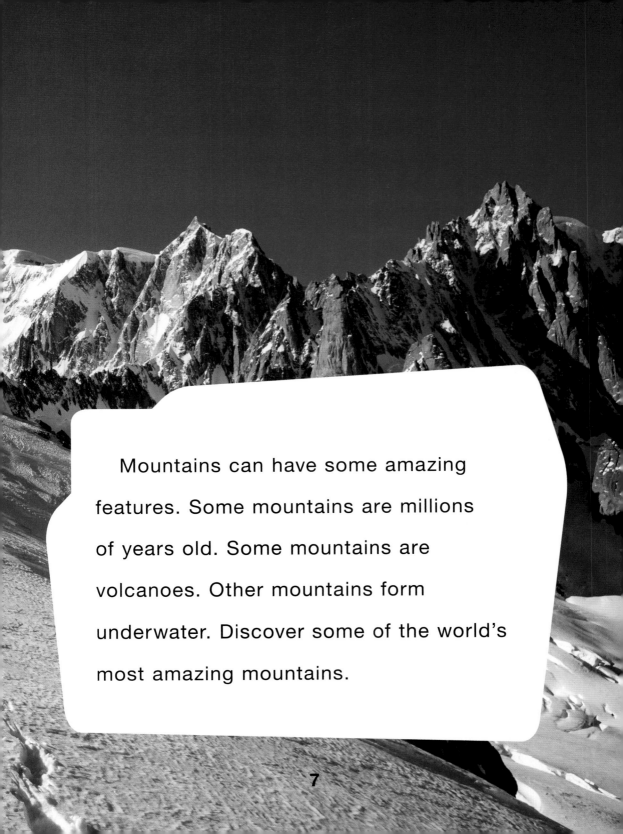

Mountains can have some amazing features. Some mountains are millions of years old. Some mountains are volcanoes. Other mountains form underwater. Discover some of the world's most amazing mountains.

CHAPTER 2

HIMALAYAS

The Himalayas are in Asia. They are the world's tallest mountains. They have many high peaks. More than 110 peaks are above 7,315 metres (24,000 feet). People from around the world climb these mountains.

The Himalayas
began to form about
50 million years ago.

Mount Everest is the highest point on Earth. It is 8,850 metres (29,035 feet) tall.

Mount Everest continues to grow every year.

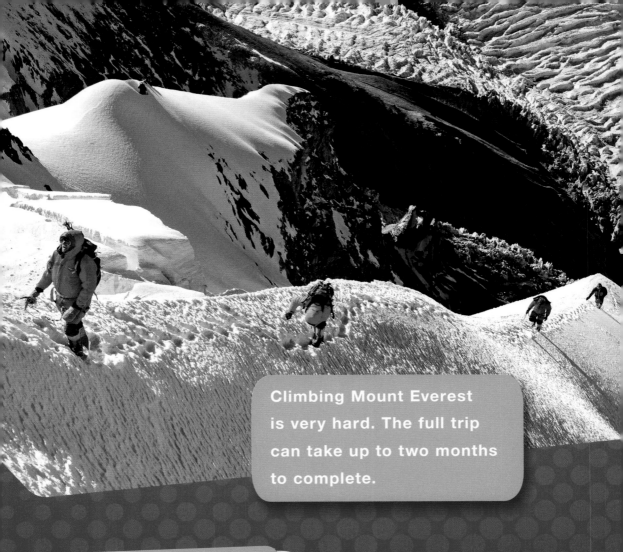

Climbing Mount Everest is very hard. The full trip can take up to two months to complete.

CLIMBERS

The youngest person to climb Mount Everest was 13 years old. The oldest was 80 years old!

CHAPTER 3

ANDES
Mountains

The Andes Mountains are in South America. They make up the world's longest mountain range. They are 7,200 kilometres (4,500 miles) long. This mountain range reaches across seven countries.

The Andean condor flies above the Andes Mountains.

There are many volcanoes in the Andes. Ojos del Salado is one of them. It is the tallest volcano in the world.

Ojos del Salado is the second-highest mountain in Chile.

15

CHAPTER 4

SIERRA Nevada

The Sierra Nevada is a large mountain range in the United States. It runs across California and part of Nevada. Mount Whitney is its highest point. It is 4,421 metres (14,505 feet) tall.

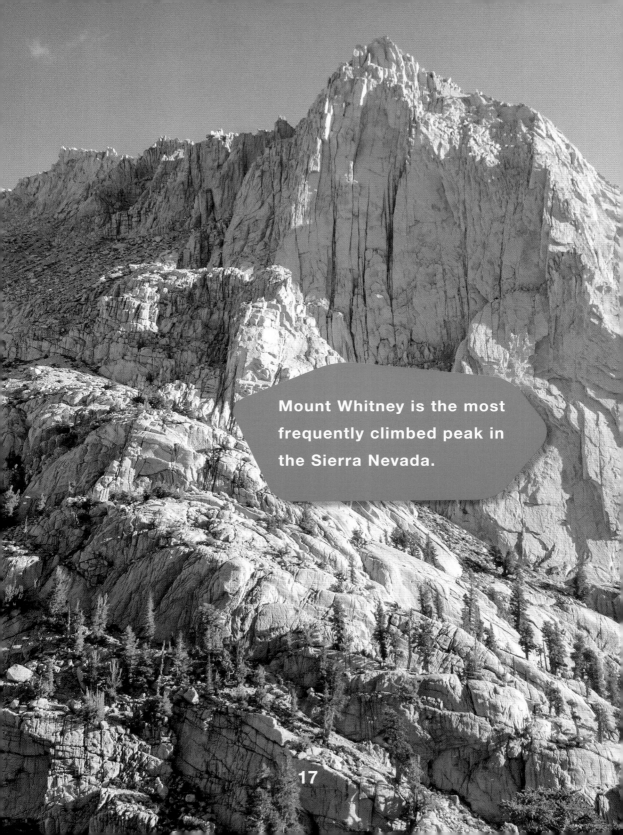

Mount Whitney is the most frequently climbed peak in the Sierra Nevada.

Giant sequoias grow on the sides of these mountains. These huge trees do not grow anywhere else. They are the largest trees in the world. They can reach more than 76 metres (250 feet) tall.

Giant sequoias can be thousands of years old.

MOUNT
Kilimanjaro

Mount Kilimanjaro is the tallest volcano in Africa. It has three **volcanic cones**. Two of these are no longer active, but one could **erupt** again one day. Nearly 25,000 people climb the mountain each year.

Elephants roam
the land below
Mount Kilimanjaro.

HAWAIIAN
Volcanoes

Mauna Loa is one of Earth's most active volcanoes. It is on the island of Hawaii, USA. It formed under the ocean long ago. Over time it grew taller and taller until it was above the water.

23

Mauna Kea is also on Hawaii. It is the highest point on the island. More than half of it is underwater. It has snow at the top and people can go skiing here!

Scientists study the stars from observatories on the top of Mauna Kea.

TALLEST MOUNTAIN

Mauna Kea is taller than Mount Everest if measured from its **base** underwater.

CHAPTER 7

MOUNT
Rushmore

Mount Rushmore is in South Dakota, USA. It is part of the Black Hills. They get their name because they look black from a distance. The highest point of the Black Hills is Black Elk Peak. It is 2,208 metres (7,244 feet) tall.

Mount Rushmore is made of a hard rock. This type of rock is good for carving. The faces of four famous US presidents are carved into the rock. Visitors come from around the world to see this amazing work.

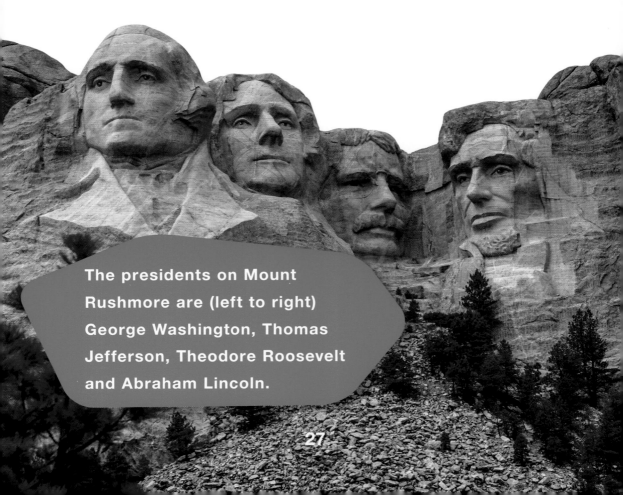

The presidents on Mount Rushmore are (left to right) George Washington, Thomas Jefferson, Theodore Roosevelt and Abraham Lincoln.

GLOSSARY

base
bottom of a mountain

erupt
when a volcano erupts, it can
blow up and spit out lava,
rocks and poisonous gases

peak
top of a mountain that comes
together at a point

plate
large piece of Earth's
outer layer (crust)

range
many mountains in a row that
are linked together

volcanic cone
hill formed of rock erupted
from a volcanic opening

TOP
MOUNTAINS
TO VISIT

ANDES MOUNTAINS, SOUTH AMERICA
Visit the longest mountain range in the world.

HIMALAYAS, ASIA
Explore the highest point on Earth.

MAUNA KEA, HAWAII, USA
Ski down this snow-covered volcano.

MAUNA LOA, HAWAII, USA
See one of the most active volcanoes in the world.

MOUNT KILIMANJARO, TANZANIA
Visit the highest mountain in Africa.

MOUNT RUSHMORE, SOUTH DAKOTA, USA
Snap photos of the presidential carvings.

MOUNT WHITNEY, CALIFORNIA, USA
See the highest peak in California.

ACTIVITY

MAKE A HOLIDAY SCRAPBOOK!

Pretend that you have recently been on a trip to the mountains. What did you pack? What did you do? What did you see? Make a scrapbook with pictures of the mountain. Cut out pictures from magazines or newspapers. Make sure you include the plants and animals you saw, and the activities you did. Next to the pictures, write a description of what happened. At the end of the scrapbook, sum up your trip. Explain why other people should visit this mountain. Then share your scrapbook with your friends.

FIND OUT MORE

Books

Exploring Mountains: A Benjamin Blog and His Inquisitive Dog Investigation (Exploring Habitats with Benjamin Blog and His Inquisitive Dog), Anita Ganeri (Raintree, 2015)

Mountains (Explorer Travel Guides), Chris Oxlade (Raintree, 2013)

Mountains and Valleys (Let's Explore Britain), James Nixon (Raintree, 2018)

Websites

www.bbc.com/bitesize/articles/z4g3qp3

Learn more about mountains and how they are formed.

www.dkfindout.com/uk/earth/mountains

Find out more about mountains.

INDEX

A Benjamin Blog
and his Inquisitive Dog
Investigation

Exploring
Mountains

Anita Ganeri

Raintree

Raintree is an imprint of Capstone Global Library Limited, a company incorporated in England and Wales having its registered office at 7 Pilgrim Street, London, EC4V 6LB – Registered company number: 6695582

www.raintreepublishers.co.uk
myorders@raintreepublishers.co.uk

Edited by Dan Nunn, Rebecca Rissman, and Helen Cox Cannons
Designed by Joanna Hinton-Malivoire
Original illustrations © Capstone Global Library Ltd
Illustrated by Sernur ISIK
Picture research by Mica Brancic
Originated by Capstone Global Library Ltd
Printed and bound in China

ISBN 978 1 406 27104 1
17 16 15 14 13
10 9 8 7 6 5 4 3 2 1

Acknowledgements
We would like to thank the following for permission to reproduce photographs: Alamy p. 15 (Mountain Light/© Galen Rowell); Getty Images pp. 5 (Raja Islam), 8 (Photodisc/Stuart Dee), 10 (Aurora/Johnathan Ampersand Esper), 22 (Nigel Pavitt), 25 (Time Life Pictures/James Burke), 26 (AFP/Namgyal Sherpa); Shutterstock pp. 6 (© mikenorton), 12 (© pinggr), 14 (© Pablo H Caridad), 17 (© Mariusz Niedzwiedzki), 18 (© Josh Schutz), 19 (© Ammit Jack), 20 (© Krom1975), 21 (© Arsgera), 23 (© Ian Woolcock), 24 (© Vixit), 27 (© Ian Woolcock), 29 top (© Roberto Cerruti), 29 bottom (© BG Smith); SuperStock pp. 4 (National Geographic/Beth Wald), 7 (Design Pics/Axiom Photographic), 9 (age fotostock), 11 (All Canada Photos/Claude Robidoux), 13 (imagebroker.net), 16 (F1 ONLINE).

Front cover photograph of a mountain landscape reproduced with permission of Shutterstock (© Pichugin Dmitry).

We would like to thank Michael Bright for his invaluable help in the preparation of this book.

Every effort has been made to contact copyright holders of material reproduced in this book. Any omissions will be rectified in subsequent printings if notice is given to the publisher.

Some words are shown in bold, **like this**. You can find out what they mean by looking in the glossary.

Contents

Welcome to the mountains!

Hello! My name's Benjamin Blog and this is Barko Polo, my **inquisitive** dog. (He's named after the ancient ace explorer **Marco Polo**.) We have just got back from our latest adventure – exploring mountains around the world. We put this book together from some of the blog posts we wrote on the way.

BARKO'S BLOG-TASTIC MOUNTAIN FACTS

Mountains are roughly more than 1,000 metres (3,333 feet) high above their surrounding area. Some are much higher – a mountain called K2, between Pakistan and China, is 8,611 metres (28,251 feet) tall – lucky I'm not scared of heights!

5

Mountain making

Posted by: Ben Blog | 20 December at 8.35 a.m.

The first stop on our trip was the Rocky Mountains in the United States. The Rockies are fold mountains. They were formed millions of years ago when two giant slabs of Earth's **crust** crashed into each other. This pushed the land in between upwards into giant folds.

6

BARKO'S BLOG-TASTIC MOUNTAIN FACTS

The Himalayas in Asia are the highest mountains on Earth. They were gradually formed after India crashed into the rest of Asia about 50 million years ago. What a sight!

Giant blocks and red-hot rocks

Posted by: Ben Blog | 25 December at 12.00 p.m.

From the Rockies, we headed across to Canada, where Barko took this photo of me in front of Mount Rundle. Mount Rundle is a block mountain. It was formed from a massive block of rock that got pushed up between two cracks in Earth's **crust**.

BARKO'S BLOG-TASTIC MOUNTAIN FACTS

Volcanoes happen when red-hot rock from deep underground comes up through cracks in Earth's crust. This is Cotopaxi in Ecuador. It hasn't **erupted** for 70 years, but I'm not going any closer, just in case!

Blowing a gale

Posted by: Ben Blog | 14 January at 3.16 p.m.

We are on the **summit** of Mount Kilimanjaro in Africa, and it's blowing a gale and freezing cold. The higher up a mountain you go, the colder it gets. That's why you get ice and snow on the top of Kilimanjaro, even though it's near the steamy **equator**.

BARKO'S BLOG-TASTIC MOUNTAIN FACTS

A blizzard is a violent snow storm that can blow up without warning. The wind blasts the snow into your face, so it's difficult to breathe or see anything. Who's there?

Knocked into shape

We arrived in the Alps this morning and headed straight for the Matterhorn on the border between Italy and Switzerland. Here's one of the photos I took. Over millions of years, the wind, water, and changes in temperature have worn the mountain into its jagged shape.

BARKO'S BLOG-TASTIC MOUNTAIN FACTS

This flat-topped mountain is near Cape Town in South Africa. It is 1,085 metres (3,559 feet) high. The wind and rain have worn it into a shape like a table. Can you guess what it's called?

13

Flowing ice, falling snow

Posted by: Ben Blog | 17 March at 4.00 p.m.

Glaciers are like gigantic rivers of ice that flow slowly down some mountain slopes. As they flow, they drag along rocks and boulders that scrape out U-shaped valleys in the mountainsides. This is the Perito Moreno glacier in Argentina. It's awesome.

BARKO'S BLOG-TASTIC MOUNTAIN FACTS

An **avalanche** is when thousands of tonnes of snow suddenly crash at high speed down a mountain. The snow buries everything in its way – trees, cars, houses, and people.

Living the high life

Animals need to be tough to live on a mountain. They have to cope with the cold, wind, snow, and steep slopes. I snapped this yak high up in the Himalayas, where it's bitterly cold. Luckily, yaks have very long, shaggy coats to keep them warm.

BARKO'S BLOG-TASTIC MOUNTAIN FACTS
Marmots in the Alps survive the winter by **hibernating** in burrows underground. They wake up again in spring, when it's warmer and there is more food around. Yawn!

17

We came across these mountain goats while we were scrambling about in the Rocky Mountains. They're brilliant at climbing, even if the slopes are very steep. Their hooves have sharp edges for digging into cracks in the rocks and pads that stop them from slipping.

BARKO'S BLOG-TASTIC MOUNTAIN FACTS

Andean condors are massive birds that soar above the slopes of the Andes Mountains in South America. They have huge wings for gliding on gusts of wind.

Sprouting slopes

Posted by: Ben Blog | 10 July at 1.00 p.m.

In summer, we headed back to the Alps to search for edelweiss. These tiny mountain plants have cleverly adapted to the cold and windy conditions. The first thing you notice about them is their furry leaves. These trap heat from the Sun and stop precious water being lost.

BARKO'S BLOG-TASTIC MOUNTAIN FACTS

High up on a mountain, you can see a treeline, or a line where trees stop growing. Above the treeline, it's too cold and windy for trees to grow.

treeline

I snapped this amazing plant in the Aberdare Mountains of Kenya, in Africa. Most mountain plants grow low to the ground to keep out of the wind, but not this giant groundsel. Giant groundsels can reach 10 metres (33 feet) high – that's about six times as tall as me.

BARKO'S BLOG-TASTIC MOUNTAIN FACTS

The splashes of colour on these rocks are tiny plant-like living things, called **lichen**. They make **acids** that **dissolve** the rocks. The lichen dig their hair-like roots into the cracks to fix themselves to the rocks.

High-rise Everest

Posted by: Ben Blog | 27 September at 6.00 a.m.

Back in the Himalayas, we are getting ready to climb Mount Everest – the highlight of our trip. It won't be easy. Mount Everest is the highest mountain on Earth – it's 8,850 metres (29,035 feet) tall. It takes several days to climb from **base camp** to the **summit**. Wish us luck!

BARKO'S BLOG-TASTIC MOUNTAN FACTS

The first people to climb Mount Everest were Edmund Hillary from New Zealand and Tenzing Norgay from Nepal. They reached the summit on 29 May 1953.

Mountains of rubbish

Posted by: Ben Blog | 2 October at 4.19 p.m.

We made it! Now it's back to **base camp** to pack up and do a quick litter pick. Mountains are brilliant places for climbing, skiing, hiking, rafting, and **paragliding**. But people are leaving tonnes of rubbish behind, and it's making a terrible mess.

BARKO'S BLOG-TASTIC MOUNTAIN FACTS
Many mountain ranges have been made into national parks to protect them. You can see these amazing rocks in the Blue Mountains National Park in Australia. Legend says that they were once three sisters who were turned into stone.

Mighty mountains quiz

If you are planning your own mountain expedition, you need to be prepared.
Find out how much you know about mighty mountains with our quick quiz.

1. What type of mountains are the Rockies?
a) fold
b) block
c) dome

2. What happens to the temperature the higher up you go?
a) it gets warmer
b) it gets colder
c) it stays the same

3. What is a **glacier**?
a) a sudden fall of snow
b) a type of mountain
c) a river of ice

4. How do yaks keep warm?
a) they **hibernate**
b) they have thick fur coats
c) they stay indoors

5. How do **lichens** break up rocks?
a) using acid
b) using hammers
c) using other rocks

6. Which is the world's highest mountain?
a) Everest
b) Kilimanjaro
c) K2

7. What is this?

8. What is this?

8. mountain goat hoofs
7. edelweiss
6. a
5. a
4. b
3. c
2. b
1. a
Answers

29

Glossary

acid liquid that breaks down rocks and other materials

avalanche sudden, massive fall of snow on a mountainside

base camp camp at the bottom of a mountain where climbers begin their climb

crust outer, rocky surface of Earth

dissolve turn something solid into liquid

equator imaginary line that runs around the middle of Earth

erupt when red-hot rock from underground comes up through cracks in Earth's crust

glacier huge river of ice that flows down a mountainside

hibernating sleeping during the winter when it is cold and there is little food about

inquisitive interested in learning about the world

lichen tiny plant-like living things that grow in crusty or bushy patches on trees and rocks

Marco Polo explorer who lived from about 1254 to 1324. He travelled from Italy to China.

paragliding sport where a person glides through the air, hanging from a wing-shaped parachute

summit top of a mountain

Find out more

Books

100 Things You Should Know about Extreme Earth, Belinda Gallagher (Miles Kelly, 2009)

Harsh Habitats (Extreme Nature), Anita Ganeri (Raintree, 2013)

Mountains (Science Kids), Margaret Hynes (Kingfisher, 2009)

The World's Most Amazing Mountains, Anna Clayborne (Raintree, 2009)

Websites

environment.nationalgeographic.com/ environment/habitats
This National Geographic website covers a range of habitats.

www.bbc.co.uk/bitesize/ks2/science/living_ things/plant_animal_habitats/read/1
Learn about habitats on this BBC website.

Index